Capitalism Stole My Virginity

Capitalism Stole My Virginity

J. Santino

Columbus, Ohio

The views and opinions expressed in this book are solely those of the author and do not reflect the views or opinions of Gatekeeper Press. Gatekeeper Press is not to be held responsible for and expressly disclaims responsibility of the content herein.

Capitalism Stole My Virginity

Published by Gatekeeper Press
2167 Stringtown Rd, Suite 109
Columbus, OH 43123-2989
www.GatekeeperPress.com

Copyright © 2022 by J. Santino
All rights reserved. Neither this book, nor any parts within it may be sold or reproduced in any form or by any electronic or mechanical means, including information storage and retrieval systems, without permission in writing from the author. The only exception is by a reviewer, who may quote short excerpts in a review.

The cover design, and editorial work for this book are entirely the product of the author. Gatekeeper Press did not participate in and is not responsible for any aspect of these elements.

Library of Congress Control Number: 2022944223

ISBN (paperback): 9781662931031

With all my love: Kelly, Oriana, and Dante

Ok, the truth of the matter is you have just bought an amazing piece of cover art from one of my favorite artists on the planet for seven to ten federal reserve notes. I have always wanted to work with this human on a project and share it with others. So here it is. I am humbled to have had the opportunity.

Artwork by: James Hattaway
JamesHattawayArt@gmail.com

Why

I was asked recently why I write, and it caught me off guard. It's just something I have always done. I paused and the first thing that came out of my mouth was, "to speak what I am not allowed to say, to come out of the closet to a place where I am no longer having to pretend to be something I am not." I would normally be focused more on short stories and nonfiction, but these times are pressing and squeezing out poems that were not intended to be shared. As for poetry, it has always been there to soothe and save me. It's a way to purge all the stimuli that enter my head daily. I never leave poetry alone for too long. I have no choice but to write poetry for my survival. I am compiling the old and new. This collection was written while living and traveling throughout Central and South America as well as the U.S. I have gathered many conversations or rants I have listened to or spoken about throughout twenty-five years as a wage laborer, a traveler, and a person like everyone with many questions. I have numerous poems on laughable pay stubs and sticky notes, and on to-do lists all scribbled on with my honest moments. Where I grew up (the southeast) is an unfortunate, beautifully intriguing place where illusion and tradition seem to hold stronger than the nature of reality as it is. I started chewing on ideas of dissent at an early age which didn't help in the institutions where I was being conditioned. I want to bring these feelings to life and not forsake them. I want to bring what each piece of scrap paper I scribbled on held as true to what people and myself were feeling in those times, so take this as you like, I will try to be faithful to those pieces of paper and wasted ink. Thank you all for coming on this journey with me.

Inside Out

The most significant
revolution is that of the
heart and mind.
Take comfort knowing what is
of the abstract,
eventually manifests itself
materially.

Eternal

One thing is sure,
what they call
forever
is futile and finite.

He Must Have Been a Mystic

It was on that rooftop in
Lima, Peru.
Our dizzy bones laid heavy
staring up at the darkest
sky.
You told me "There is
meaning."
I said,
"Show me."
You played the most
enchanting song,
breathing life into every
note.
Then we watched as they
wandered up into the heavens,
sat as stars and lit up our
sacred rooftop
and frightened souls like
magic.

Yo Deseo A Colombia

I came for love,
I stayed for the piss poor
beer
and depressing vallenato.

In The Margins

When you esteem others
greater
than yourself,
love others
and want the same for them as
you do for you
and your family, there will
be holy trouble.
You will, with great love,
find yourself on the outside
of the ruthless norm,
the glass house that
encompasses so many.
Throw rocks at that glass
house,
break out holes of hope.
Love so hard you get in
trouble for it.

For Real

I don't recall a good love
story that didn't involve
anarchy.

Holy Water

Grasp me tight.
Commence the dance,
the hydrophilic parade.
Welcome in the summer storms
to wash our souls clean.
Hold that frequency,
gnash my teeth.
Take root in the fertile soil
beneath the power lines.
Hear the locust sing their
apocalyptic hymns.
Set the precedence, rejoice
in the shedding of our skin.

Always Together

You are the embodiment of
adventure.
You are the escape that I
craved since grade school.
We crossed borders illegally
and ran through jungles
far,
far away.
You are liberation.

Just Maybe

"There must be something about the meaningless that is beautiful," I said.

She told me, "Together we can figure it out." Then everything had meaning.

No Such Thing as a Stranger

Do what you will with your
human experience,
just try to take some time to
wash each other's feet.

Drive

You know I love nights,
long rides
with nowhere to go.
From paved to dirt canopy
roads.
These trees watched us grow
and the stars followed us
till we were home.
You know I love killing
ambition,
and filling up
on passion
alone.

Class War

I am in my rowboat paddling
away,
so, hope looks like saddling
on dismay.
At pace with the next current
to another galaxy,
as I am staring at my
landlord in the face.
Beams arrogance, seems no
matter what argument is
logical or good for an
apologetical foundation is in
vain.
It's a seed sprung from
systemic delusion,
confusion nourished by the
macabre of allegiance,
now standing as mommy's proud
little sociopath.

Direction

He told me he sees signs from
the universe.
I just see signs telling me
to buy shit.

Killearn Vs the CO-OP

On every piece of cement, we skateboarded.
Every patch of grass we wrestled.
Our scabbed arms and legs, our sweat soaked,
grass-stained clothes, all testified of our love for one another and determination to make everything count.
Every night we laid storytelling waiting to greet the moon.

No Land in Sight

The stars do not shine
tonight,
they have taken dim in
reverence of your departure.
I am left with your
silhouette in my head
illuminated red from the port
side running light.
It was an honor at sea to
share one last cigarette.

No Thanks

We joined the choir of rocks
and trees long before hills
wrote songs for profit,
and chapels elevated.

Ins and Outs of the Omnipresent

Traveling dimensions,
I am bereft of nothing.
I wonder if these creatures
ponder the ego.
I sit silently for billions
of years waiting,
hoping for the living and the
dead ones.
When all material vanishes,
there is still the One who
remains ever present in life
and death.

Love Well

Being a living sacrifice
hurts way more than being a
dead one. The world does not
teach sacrificial love
because it's not comfortable
or conditional,
like the things we crave. And
well, it hurts. It knows no
boundaries or self. It often
operates in pain and
discomfort and is
entwined with faith.
Oh, it changes the world!

Reason

We do not live a meaningless experience,
while giving meaning to it,
while not meaning to.

Fallen

It fell from the sky,
hit the earth,
and shattered into a plume of
stained glass,
an intense luminance.
We curiously gathered the
warm,
polished pieces of color as
they battered about us.
We cherished them as the
vestiges of the last chapel
to teach love and compassion.

Love VS the World

Now, I'm starting to see why
ole Johnny was content on a
diet of locust and honey.
Now, only a polaroid can
catch truth. (smile)
I crashed my car into a river
named Jordan and haven't been
the same since.
Everything seems upside down.
The must-haves,
the things declared
important,
the success they teach
all seems so fruitless.
Now, hope is so much sweeter
in the things unseen.

Mi Vida

Genetic prototype,
production of unconditional
love and chaos.
Sacrificial living flows easy
with your essence
and
nature since you first
arrived.

Gilles De La Tourette

I buried the mask,
pulled away, and started
anew.
Singing with the coyotes,
swarming with the cicadas.
Shaking scales off my eyes.
Turn up the impulses on this
deep brain stimulation.
Strange dystonia
overwhelming,
only relived by pain amongst
the clouds.
Through the pines and spanish
moss my electricity fades,
synapses dictate this painful
dance.
Inhale the barometric low,
grasp for control. Try again
tomorrow.

Search & No Rescue

The flies swarm in
procession,
the radio speaks in static
tongues.
Hold fast, here comes another
wave.
I swear this part of the sea
is hexed.
You are not my first and
won't be my last.
Stay calm,
stay lifeless,
we will return you home.
Your family waits at the pier
with handkerchiefs heavy with
tears.
It was a pleasure to meet
you.
I will be wherever you are
soon.

Conductor

And here comes that substance
again.
Just when I thought I was
losing it.
A supernatural glue that
holds my soul to this flesh.
The soul,
the receiver,
the transmitter that connects
me, connects us all.
It satisfies
and keeps me ever connected
to your love.

Out of Ink

A whole life,
an introspective plethora of
self-sustenance, self-pity,
self-praise,
self-loathing,
self,
self, self. How foolish to
say you
worship nothing?
Beloved, you worship, you
give praise. The thing is you
always
worshiped yourself.

Todo Amor

You know I'm always stuck in
my head,
playing with words,
and meaning,
always trying on situations.
You know I'm never out of
words. I use them as a
defense from my insecurities.
I mix in any conversation
well, and hate them all.
I am scared, so I speak.
Everyone thinks I'm happy to
be apart,
really,
I'm just scared.
I camouflage myself in
conversation.
Only you can fill me up,
to a point of complete
silence and contentment.
Only you can break me out of
my head,
to a point where I am
comfortable in complete
silence.

CEO

Blistered palms, carry on,
carry on.
They lay in homes they could
not build,
nor clean, nor fill.
Sweaty brows,
carry on, carry on.
Oh, so well they lay in
luxury and
savor, always knowing
their workers
could never
be their neighbor.

Never Stop Rambling

Let's go to new places,
experience new things far
away from here.
If people are truly created
in the image of God,
I want to meet them all.

Prescribed

She could not be summoned.
She had love to give,
but none to receive.
She smiled relentlessly but
was never truly amused.
She was a bittersweet
tincture that only lasted so
long.

No refills authorized.

Bienvenidos A Estados Unidos

We are mourning,
but medicated.
Our faces stuck in a similar
rictus,
troubled yet comfortable,
adjusted.
Grieving in sackcloth made
by the finest designers.
We are not ok,
but somehow,
we still obey.
Just another second then we
will be entertained.
Maybe another celebrity to
save us?
Oh wait, a couple more days
and we get paid.

Faith and Shuffleboard

It was a good night if we
didn't have to put our hands
on anyone.
This was our spot,
our little sanctuary.
It smelled of stale beer,
puke
and
yeast infections.
Filled with bikers,
transients gutter punks
and suicidal businessmen.
Father Pedro loved the
shuffleboard as did I.
He always won.
This is where we discussed
the holiest of things,
the unseen,
the heavenly glories,
and
sweet grace.
He had the spirit and
operated in its freedom.
I was still just drowning in
dogma
and cheap wine.

Love, Romance, and Ketamine

Neuro divergent - time travel
prescribed.
Flew past the unwilling
participants for eugenic
sacrifices.
Scraped the concrete
and jumped on the vertical
train heading straight
upwards.
Hope and pray
I'll be able to find a ride
down.
Would you mind if I tag
along?
I'm healing up now
and want to hold you in the
waking world,
would you mind?
We can love freely till we
feed the soil and produce
sacred shade
for all to find rest and
comfort.
Would you mind?

Convalesce

I picked a brick from Babylon
made from moral turpitude.
Maybe it can be as an epitaph
for the admonition of useless
servitude.
Building a splendid rendition
from intuition learned
through the spirit and human
condition.
My pockets are full of false
pretense,
sand,
and
sludge.
If I may,
can I come over now?
I am stuck in a hard place
between love,
poetry,
and prose.
Everyone keeps screaming
from comfortable omission
saying, "that's just how it
goes!"

Over It

Find something worth dying
for,
especially in a sick world
that thinks and teaches there
are things worth killing for.
We weave in and out of this
threadwork.
Ever changing,
never changing.
Iteration of monotonous
living,
always taking.
I don't have much more to
offer to that structure.
I am running fast, leaving
the dust from my feet
behind me, enjoy it.
I find my way by losing it.
I begin living by dying.
Build community by rejecting
it as it stands. I'm bouncing
off determinism
and free will, both are

excruciating. Take my bags, I have no need for them anymore.
Take my place, it was never mine to begin with.

Back to the Empire

These wings are flying me
home heartbroken.
Prepare for takeoff,
no,
please,
I'll open the exit door!
I need the right seat.
More tv dinners, name-it,
claim-it preachers
and motivational speakers.
I'll lose it if I hear
another "Barnum sentence."
Mundane production serves a
few.
24-hour news
eclipsed by the rattling from
the brood of diamondbacks,
emergency broadcast.
I got nine lives and five
sides to every open wound.
Black powder bangs
for the most meaningless race
to ensue.

Vitality

And there she stood,
charred,
and burnt.
Some edges seared off.
A smile so honest and big,
showing off her teeth
covered in soot.
Hermosa,
I thought,
knowing she had just made it
through hell.

Ride

The pavement passes by at
light speed.
These live oaks have so many
stories to tell, and they
tell them well.
Wound wood and regrowth.
Scars on giants,
scabs are worn proud in
reverence.
Lights flash and we walk on
shards of glass
in an epileptic hell just to
find death.

Here & There

Only here can you paint the
galaxy with one brushstroke
and
exhale a genus of orchids.
Only here every movement
brings about angelic song.
Take a swim,
And jump right in.
Lose everything for just a
time.
Find out there is no place
between space and time.
Let it heal you.
Give up the civility for just
a moment so you can breathe.
Jump in.

Psalm For the Wet Season

From her front porch we
always threw smiles back and
forth.
I always wondered if you
could even leave.
Her eyes always matched the
changing of the skies.
I always questioned if you
could love me the way I loved
you,
without a word ever spoken.
It was pouring rain on the
hottest Nicaraguan day
when I heard her at my door,
standing soaking wet with her
father's pale horse.
We rode and galloped through
the yuca fields until
I couldn't hold my love back
anymore.

Function

Everything functions better
with love over hierarchy.

Tomorrow

I'm looking for yesterday
because tomorrow is looking
at me strange.
I miss those volcanic
eruptions
and
late-night swims on Lake
Granada.
I'm missing breaking out
streetlights at dusk.
The sweaty bed sheets
and the smell of morning
breath.
Besides the memory, where
does yesterday reside?

Birdsong

Even the birds are singing
off-key.
The grass is bleeding.
I sing along trying to
harmonize.
I eat fertilizer and piss in
the weeds.
I pray for rain.
I need it to clean me once
again.
A cardinal watches me from my
window sill as I try to lift
my head from my pillow.
I watch it burst into flames
while flying away,
leaving a trail of fine,
red powder pigment floating
to and fro.
Suddenly, everything
comes into harmony.
Everything
brings gratitude and praise.

After

I'm terrified of heights.
I hate the feeling of
falling, but
I have no qualms with hitting
the ground.

Gone

We had been driving in
circles through this endless
maze of roads and broken
homes for hours.
We have lived here over
twenty years
but had no clue where we
were.
The streetlights looked
familiar and
blinding.
He was strangling the
steering wheel wide-eyed.
I couldn't feel my hands.
We erratically skid to a
screeching halt.
He looked at me trembling.
"We must get the hell outta
here."
We still didn't know where
here was.
And the rest of our lives we
have been trying to get the
hell out of here.

Catch a Breeze

We both moved with the wind.
We both had the same vision
and craved one another.
We flew up and down with the
thermals around the universe.
We wanted to stay together.
We just never again caught
the same breeze.

Look

We ran in packs like wolves.
We were scavengers addicted
to grotesque adventures,
ones that freed us from time.
People hated our presence and
mocked our existence.
We were proud to be their
scum,
their very creation.
We bathed in disapproval,
took
shelter in abandoned
buildings and
ran naked on rooftops.
We watched the charade from
the clouds.
Fancy people pretending,
playing,
lying to themselves.
They had forged smiles on
their faces,
and played all the
meaningless games very well.
It was better on the
rooftops.

It was better as scum.

We had found something
magical on those buildings
and would die for it.
We had found ourselves or
lost ourselves.
I still don't know what
either means.

Nice to meet you

I met a girl named Serenity
in a nowhere bar in
Nicaragua.
She killed her stepdad in
Texas.
"Mean abusive son of a
bitch," she said.
She killed a fortune teller
in New Orleans, after he told
her life had good things in
store for her.
"Mean abusive son of a
bitch," she said.
She was elegant in a strange
country way.
She seemed to float as she
walked effortlessly.
She transcended my
defenses and I was
immediately,
helplessly in love.
I told her I loved her.
"You're a mean abusive son of
a bitch," she said.
They buried me behind the
bar.

Final

I was on my last dime.
I felt like a prize fighter's
last check.
The last drag of a cigarette
before a meteor hits.
The sun is mocking and on
loop.
Let's put something in the
air while we still have one
another.
Let's risk it all.
You know I love dancing on
thin ice.

Bemoan

Sanctuary of jackals
embracing us.
Unrecognized bones,
stricken
fruits.
The hands kindle fire.
False prophets shed blood.
Touch us!
Joy waits,
thrown down
and torn.
Forgive us!
Harvest everything
in the
crumbling of the nations,
rightly so.
Save us!

Love is Power

It's those strange ones,
whose souls are so heavy
and anchored with love
and sacrifice.
The world loves to kill them,
but they never really leave.
It is death as a catalyst.
What they have started can
never be stopped.
You were one of those
beautifully strange ones.

Medellin Love Story

Our favorite breakfast place,
we would sit under pictures
of
Jesus the Nazarene,
Bolivar,
and
Zapata.
They gave our bones
confidence,
courage
and hope for things anew.
We shared our languages,
our food,
our flesh,
even the car exhaust that
lingered in the air tasted
sweet with you.
My new morning ritual of
love, for you.
Every morning we sat in silly
love brand new.
I swear there was no better
view…
No,
not one better than you.

Anew

What nation state lives on
when the seed was infected,
and the roots only feed on
death and destruction?
Manifest destiny produces
empires ready for toppling.
What kinds of fruits did you
think we would produce?
We need an axe for the tree
and the roots.

Swamp

Floating face up in this swamp,
stargazing.
The enchantments of the sirens brought me here.
I'm a sucker for song.
Protected by the arms of the cypress trees
and the bullfrog on my belly.
I was baptized in this swamp,
and no one ever pulled me up.
Saint Frances took a vow of poverty,
I guess somewhere along this assembly line
I started to understand why,
and it seems we all took a vow to be a commodity.
Dissociation became my highest form of education.
As for now I'll just stay here floating,
marinating in metaphors and hesitation.
As for the swamp, till death do us part.

Growth

It's the martyrs that ignite
sweeping loving change.
The killers look foolish and
bring shame.
So, dance,
sing and rejoice in the face
of cowards. There is not a
human alive
you should fear.
Don't give them that power
and control.
Honestly,
fuck em.

We Are Now Free to Be

I found a way to write and
get paid,
it's while my bosses are
distracted,
drooling over the bottom line
and
the females in short skirts.
I work for self-proclaimed
patriots
outsourcing work overseas for
slave wages.
I'm stuck trying to figure it
out.
I am useless like a book with
no pages.
I am an actor that never
broke any legs and-keeps
praying things can be
different,
not for my sake,
but our children.
Let's save them!

Palm Sunday 2050

The buzzards are circling
your board rooms again.
Hide your shareholders.
The peasants
and proletariats are in the
streets throwing spears at
your chariots.
Can't let the pestilence
perpetuate.
The lures in your tackle box
no longer look palatable.
Exhausted with the spectacle.
Warning we are concerned with
truth and reason again.
Your stallions died in vain
and litter the roadsides.
Our turn to welcome in the
donkey that needs no reins.

Biblical Grade Ergot

I fell into the meadow after
being scalped by a ring of
Saturn.
I lay punch drunk staring at
a burning
bush,
or maybe
it's a building.
I was stung by the sun
and touched by celestial
hands.
I rest and wait for any sign
of life to light my soul
afire.
I need your breath of life.
It's the only life left.

Different Textures of Feces

A liberal is just another
capitalist
with a coexist bumper
sticker,
we ain't fooled.

Mr. Solomon was not Messing Around

Farewell,
we sing your eulogy.
We have been left with
useless supply side
economics-can we get a link?
It has raised our latchkey
children well.
Now we are nothing more than
adults sitting in diapers
full of a digested life
lived for trivialities.
We have accomplished
everything prescribed
and with no satisfaction
and it only served a few.
Nothing is achieved,
vanity!
Stuck in a static state of
apathy,
pretending our production is
useful
but it just benefits the few.

Selfish,
never changing.
I swear I just saw another
apparition,
she appeared on Wall Street
wearing a Rolex on her wrist
and money in her fist.
Goodbye sweetie,
this is no longer my home.

Words Spoken at Night

Patriotism,
fine have at it.
As for nationalism,
it will always lead to
ethnocentricity,
blind obedience,
destruction,
and death.
It always hinders mental
and
spiritual growth.
The unsettling reality is you
can have patriotism without
nationalism,
but you cannot have
nationalism
without patriotism.

Day

Our souls were connected
and working before we ever
met.
O'what a day,
what a day for reflection.
Can you taste the sound of
joy?
Touch the complexion of
infatuation.
Can you smell the frequency
of adulation? I just want to
be where you are, it really
is that simple.

Listen

The silence is like a train
whistle in my ear.
The dead do speak
and it's too loud.
Justice comes toothless.
The roses reek,
smell them!
Ruthless are the days paved
with golden illusions.
Hold in that breath, you'll
need it.
Protect your chest, your heat
is leaking out.
Birds are falling from the
sky again,
people pleading to be seen
not just heard.
I see you!
Let me carry that for you.
Let me even the load, the
burden,
yours is mine.
We will bury it deep in the

earth,
deep enough that it will
never resurrect
and creep back up.

No one should ever carry that
burden alone.

Closer Look

Please allow us to serve you.
We are casting lots for the
have-nots.
Throwing pennies in
bottomless tombs,
wishing in wells,
pulling up the finest water
to bottle
from the artesian reservoirs
from Flint, Michigan.
I begin to feel again that
passion scraping through my
veins
like liquid sandpaper.
Faster now!
The energy is manic
and necessary,
it causes the sub to burst.
I unrolled the scroll,
tried to read it out loud,
got tongue-tied.
The ink lifted from the paper
and the words took form,

molded into functional
destruction of discourse to
make way for loving action,
it's the only change we've
seen that's not ephemeral.
Days of risible old bones
congregating for ideas are
almost over.
Derelict rhetoric
soon extinct.

Purge

He stood next to me at Chairs
Crossroads projectile
vomiting straight down.
When he got a breath,
he looked at me and screamed,
"pick up the bones."
We sifted and waded through
the acidic muck.
"Take the bones, they are the
only things left of me," he
said.
He purged everything right
there in the middle of those
lonely roads.
Everything he had ever
learned,
believed,
loved,
and held as true, sat in
the pool of stench.
"What's with the bones?"
I asked.
He just looked at me and
laughed.

Ofrenda

She offended the offering by
contending for holiness.
She couldn't grasp the bloody
reality of sacrifice.
She is lovely,
she is chosen,
she dances bewitchingly.
She spits venom in the lava
just to watch it boil.
She slowly disperses into
lustrous embers,
carried away with the wind
and lands in all seven seas.
Her journey is just beginning,
it's a transcendence of being
now, an oceanic ride. A deep
dive into a subaquatic
undertaking.
The earth shakes,
tsunamis take form,
and they dance their storms
to all earth's shores.

Making Way

The cacophony of screaming
silence is shaking these
graves.
The centipede bites cover our
bodies as we set sail.
Fair winds and following seas
as we skip
across mother ocean.
We packed all the charts,
and
enough
corrosives
and
explosives
for a perfect burial at sea.
We will anchor on the leeward
side of Hope Island.
This area is mystical,
haunted
and
perfect for you.
It is what you always dreamed
of being and now, you will be.

Struggle

Learning to bask in the gratitude,
to lean into it like a strong wind.
Lean in, especially in the valleys because even in the deaths of soggy despair in the valleys you can still look up and see the majestic mountain peaks.

Calling

Now here is the hard part.
When you start to realize
that most of those around you
on a very constant basis are
not by choice.
We can't choose our coworkers
or
those who happen to have
found their way into our
well-worn paths.
Most outside of your sacred
circle do not feel for you.
They might even be an enemy.
Now,
learn to love them!
Not just for your sake,
but all of humanity.

Mark

You first reported trembling.
It wasn't long before you had
got accustomed to life at
sea.
Everyone loved you.
Your smile
lifted rooms
and calmed storms.
Your dreams were many
and
they always sat behind your
eyes.
We practiced knots,
drank whisky,
spliced lines,
and fought all comers.
It was the dog and pony show
that got to you.
The despicable men
and
women did not
believe in you.
We believed in you.

You built your grave on the
bridge right next to those
deplorable,
decorated officers.
Medals shinning in the light
of destruction.
We believed in you.
Your courage to stand in the
face of evil was remarkable.
Your grave on the top of the
ship serves as a beacon of
hope
for those
of us not so courageous.
We needed more of you,
but you had nothing left to
give.
We now
have nothing left to lose.

Was a Hell of a Poet

At this universal juncture,
loving everyone as yourself
is an act of rebellion.
She was revolutionary in that
way,
and
revolutionaries appear to
create some of the greatest
poetry.
She was poetry.

An Aside

As it stands,
todo amor
torn by war.
No pledge of allegiance to
anything made by human hands,
not anymore,
we stopped
keeping score.
Death race
set up by many martinets,
arsonist become heroes
making candles out of
narcissist,
targetless,
lighting the way.
Gene pools
machine fools into flowing
streams that rule
with botulism,
not a place left for
altruism.
Not a space left except the
gap in the schism.

Prison,
complex organisms
seems promised
and welcomed,
cast stones
to sell them what they need.
All agreed what they give is
what we need.
Planetary needs
refused,
swallowed by greed.
Binary states of being
controlled by mutated
advisory.
Eyes blinded by bribery,
what a sight to see.
We'll all gather it up and
send it back
through the refinery to
start the process,
part the obstacles
and be
reborn in our entirety.

Sleepwalk

This must be some type of
paradoxical sleep,
but
I still have muscular
control.
I sleep talk,
sleepwalk.
I feel the weight heavy upon me.
I think I just saw King David
on the third lap making our
beds swim.
I remember what it's like to
feel to heal.
I am thrown down but remain
grateful.
I heal,
then break,
and
fracture again
my brittle bones.
I'm in the depths.
I walk the silent streets.
I pick the scab to heal once

again,
I like the way it feels.
Grateful,
painful,
no control.
I surrender again
because that starts the
saving process.
Its name is Chorea
I am wrapped in a body
I
can
not
control.

Rise

Succulent are the lips that
suck the air from my lungs.
Graceful are the hips that
lead the dance.
Beautiful are the days that
bring you over.
Gorgeous are the years
growing into one.
I awake and find my life in
yours.

Poetry Saves

Too young, but felt I should
not be here.
I stayed talking,
joking anything to disguise
myself.
Something was in the painful
process of conception in all
of me.
I continued to hide
as I was
coming undone.
Love was there somewhere,
I just couldn't grasp it.
Something was coming,
I was clueless, I had not
heard the whispers clearly.
I laughed as I was being
unhinged.
Quick to lose the temper,
quick to find it.
Young with bloody swollen
gums.

Too young to know what was coming.
Rung dry,
sleep deprived,
consciously
unconscious,
lucid,
dissonance,
repentance.
A few journeys later,
and there it was.
Poetry came and nothing has been the same.
It just took time and pain.

Grace

My heart beats, pounds the
pavement in the streets.
Born breech landed on my feet
running to love you,
to serve you.
I'm running for your glory
because of your grace.
Let me keep running through
your fields
and
wildfires.
Let it all give you glory.

Khuba

Your love is a subversive
love.
It's a table-flipping love.
Your love starts
inextinguishable fires that I
crave to dwell in.

Working Class Proverb

Once we truly invest in
carrying one another's
burdens,
the governing bodies
and the
owning class will start to
lose their suffocating grip.
In this powerful love the
illusion starts to fade,
and that
scares the hell outa them.
And when they look around and
have no one else to exploit,
we will forgive, love and
welcome them too.

Shake

Blood from every Caesar is
being collected in gutters of
the suburban cul-de-sacs.
Snack packs and flags for
rags.
I am writing love notes on
toe tags.
Mutation of spiritual
inflation rises from the
dusty roads.
I am left out in the cold,
hold my soul, froze.
Grow back my limbs whole.
Circling with the clouds,
using the same polyphonic
sounds that brought the walls
of Jericho down.
It's all coming round.
It's all coming down.

You

I am so sorry, I just sit and
smile.
No words penned
nor spoken
can explain of your
beautifully
chaotic existence.
Sometimes silence is the most
profound expression.

Exist

Been walking for years.
No bags,
food,
or compass.
Oneness fled for justice.
All cuisine is provided by my
guillotine.
It's breaking down but still
makes the cut.
Gutless,
fed on roadkill
and the future looking
sunless.
Iteration of the monotonous
ambition condition.
You got this; you can break
this cyclical tragedy.
You are pixel perfect,
stop just surviving,
you can do more than exist.

Go

I'll travel any road as long
as I don't know where
it goes.

Alive

"We are almost there,
keep following.
I know this forest well.
Did you bring the sacrifice
that could never suffice?
This is where we see it,
this is holy ground remove
your shoes,"
she said, as she gazed at it
with intensity,
then towards the sky and
screamed, "we are alive!" I
had no clue what she meant.

Choke

This is the whole unbreakable
wishbone.
This is the flower that never
stops blooming.
This is Joseph's brothers
grooming him for death,
consuming greed,
jealousy holding hands with
entropy.
This is me holding a rock in
a sock,
stuck in the line at the
marketplace of ideas that
seems out of stock.
This is the last cup of wine
from the wedding at Canaan.
Way past time, now it
never stops raining, except
when a new vine is grafted
in.
Fasted at a motel.
I'm
shrinking!

No more shell,
no rooms at the inn.
Stuck,
no luck.

This is hovering in space,
the last place left for
grace.
Watching commercials in
between weaving smoke
circles.
This is not seeing, it's
believing, because everything
I can touch fades away.
Everything material is as
such, and that includes
today.

Connection

That day holds on,
although it's dead and gone.
That smell arises
sporadically and vague,
hello condemnation.
Those eyes went deeper than
mother ocean. They held the
seasons changing, the tides
shifting, the earth-shaking,
they held peace and war. They
were prophetic windows of
everything that
came to be.

My inspiration

I hold your art,
your smile, and keep your
words written on my heart.
All of it has attached itself
to my soul.
I took our time for granted.
I take all time for granted.
I thought you'd always be
around.
I couldn't have imagined a
life living in your absence.
Here I am,
still hoping to catch another
dream about you,
a smell,
a memory,
a song anything that brings
me into a sweet,
surreal connection with you.
That's all I get now,
but it keeps me going.

Color upon color

We had dreams more colorful
than hot air balloons on
fire.
Leaving soon,
marking off days of
dissonance from the calendar.
Adventurer,
still ready to ride with the
crew of the Challenger.
Speak softly,
move with intention and
listen.
Transcending to the land of
the Messiah,
hands burnt by this celestial
compass.
Take the reins of this
asteroid,
all I need is my sacred
cutlass.
Spirits scream, turbulent
means.
Hope gleams in lucid dreams,
looking through the perfect
prism for space-time fabric
seams.

Iconoclast

He showed me comfort in pain,
and beauty in suffering.
He flipped the empire on its
head and the rich felt the
weight of their existence.
Nothing they had was through
persistence, just theft.
Take a heavy breath.
My teeth grind with the
clock. I can't stop watching
time. Can't stop breaking my
neck.
I saw liberation from toil
and that it all goes rotten
and spoils.

Long gone

Tithes are now just bribes
for puppets behind pulpits to
keep their mouths sewn shut.
It's the new wave to not even
be able to call a spade a
spade.
Darker days for the
downtrodden who can't find
words of rest.
The words of the prophets and
preachers are now against the
oppressed.

Climb

Just basking in gratitude
even in the valleys,
especially in the muddy
valleys, because there you
can still look up and see the
majestic peaks.

Feel free to contact me anytime, for anything.
Thank you for your loving support.

I.G @wordsbysantino
wordsbysantio@gmail.com

www.ingramcontent.com/pod-product-compliance
Lightning Source LLC
LaVergne TN
LVHW011727060526
838200LV00051B/3065